A Fruit Of The Spirit Cocktail

Tracey Laster

Archway Publishing books may be ordered through booksellers or by contacting:

Archway Publishing
1663 Liberty Drive
Bloomington, IN 47403
www.archwaypublishing.com
844-669-3957

Interior Image Credit: U.K. Roy

All Scripture quotations are taken from the King James Version.

ISBN: 978-1-6657-1000-8 (sc)
ISBN: 978-1-6657-1001-5 (hc)
ISBN: 978-1-6657-0999-6 (e)

Print information available on the last page.

Archway Publishing rev. date: 08/06/2021

Galatians 5:22 KJV

But the fruit of the Spirit is love, joy, peace, longsuffering, gentleness, goodness, faith, meekness, temperance: against such there is no law.

In our bowl of Fruit of the Spirit Cocktail, we have an Apple; Banana, Pineapple, Honeydew, Cantaloupe, Watermelon, Peach, Strawberries and Grapes!

John 3:16 KJV

For God so loved the world, that he gave his only begotten Son, that whosoever believeth in him should not perish, but have everlasting life.

Apple is for Love

Ayannah loves her Nana and
Papa with all her heart!

James 1:2 KJV

My brethren, count it all joy when
you fall into divers temptations;

Grapes are for Joy

Laila was filled with joy to hear she would be visiting her relatives soon.

Proverbs 15:1 KJV

A soft answer turneth away wrath:
but grievous words stir up anger.

Banana is for Gentleness

Their Mom spoke with a soft gentle voice to her husband.

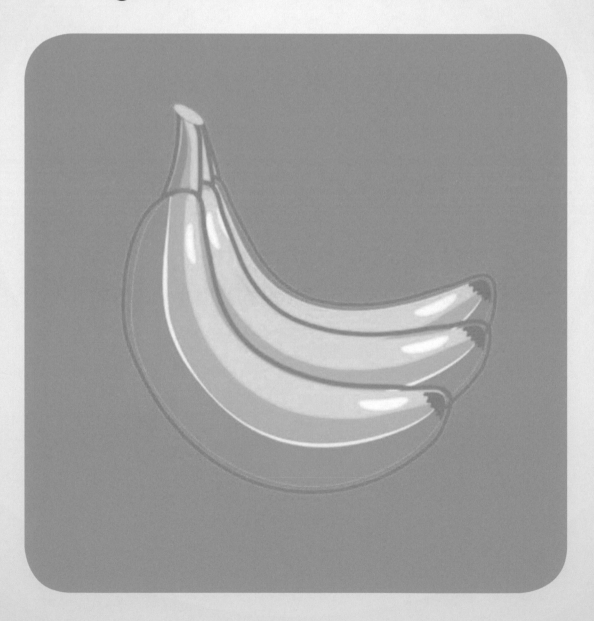

Lamentations 3:25 KJV

The Lord is good unto them that wait for him, to the soul that seeketh him.

Strawberries are for Goodness

It was good of Malia to share
her toy with Myles.

Matthew 5: 5 KJV

Blessed are the meek: For they shall inherit the earth.

Pineapple is for Meekness

Ethan was chosen by his classmates because of his meekness.

Psalm 4:8 KJV

I will both lay me down in peace, and sleep: for thou, Lord, only makest me dwell in safety.

Peach is for Peace

The students had a peaceful game though they were on different teams.

Psalms 86:15 KJV

"But thou, O Lord, art a God full of compassion, and gracious, longsuffering, and plenteous in mercy and truth."

Honeydew is for Longsuffering

Michaela endured longsuffering while waiting for her little brother to come out of the bathroom.

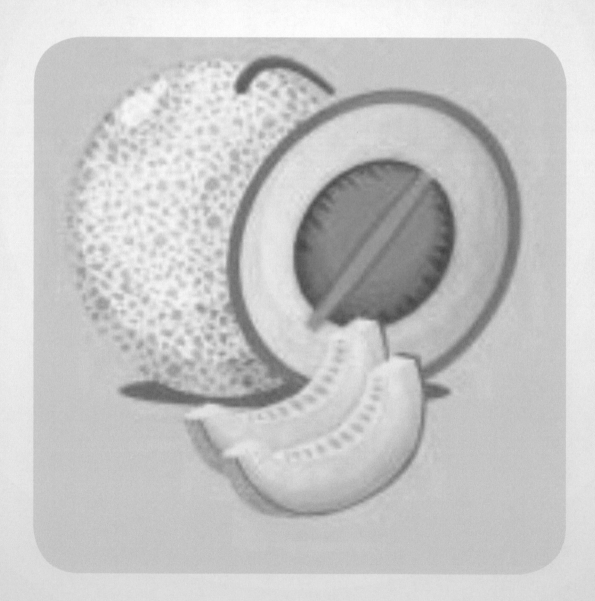

2 Peter 1:16 KJV

And to knowledge temperance;
and to temperance patience;
and to patience godliness;

Cantaloupe is for Temperance

Brent presented temperance when Michaela accidentally hit him with the ball.

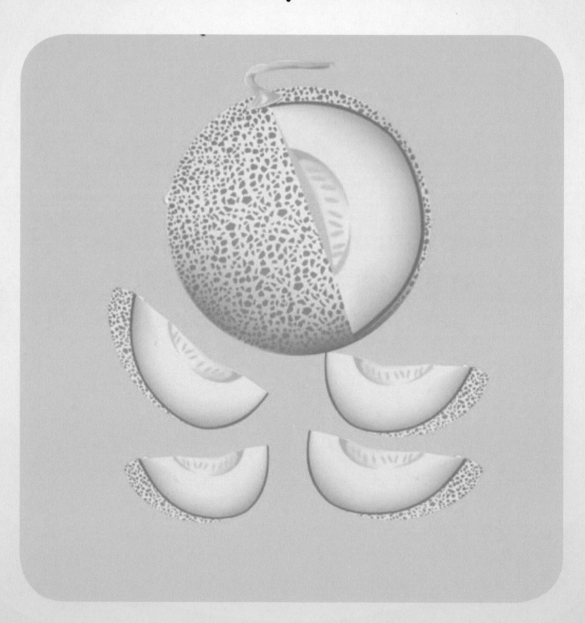

Hebrews 11:1 KJV

Now faith is the substance of things hope for, the evidence of things not seen.

Watermelon is for Faith

Ava was excited she got the gift she was hoping for on her birthday!

By eating these natural nutritious fruits on a regular basics, you will grow up to be strong and healthy.

You will have strong bones and teeth. Healthy hair, nails and skin. You will look amazing!

Likewise, if you take in the fruit of the spirit your character will grow to be strong and beautiful too.

Your appearance will become brighter! You will draw others closer to you. They will love your spirit and want to be just like you.

Don't just eat one of the fruits and not the others. You will miss out on a lot of nutrients that the other fruits have.

You have to mix them all together in a cocktail so you will get a variety of different flavors and nutrients.

Likewise, you can't show meekness and not have love or have plenty of joy and no faith.

You will have to walk in all the fruit of the spirit. It will not happen overnight.

It's a growing process but I
promise if you keep working on
yourself you will get there.

When you eat an apple love for yourself and others will grow. A bundle of grapes will produce lots of joy. A gentle spirit will live in you after eating a banana.

Strawberries will help you become good to everyone you meet. While the sweet taste of a pineapple will help develop the spirit of meekness. You will possess peace while munching on a juicy peach.

While indulging in the great flavors of a honeydew, you will build up a tolerance for longsuffering. A cantaloupe is sweet and juicy too and will be a great help for tolerance. Add the watermelon to build up your faith!

A Fruit of the Spirit Cocktail can be eaten by all boys and girls no matter who you are or where you are from.

You can share The Fruit of the
Spirit Cocktail with your parents,
siblings and friends.

I know you will certainly love the delicious taste of the fruits in the bowl of Fruit of the Spirit Cocktail.

I promise you will also love the
characteristic hidden in each
of the fruit of the spirit.

While becoming healthy boys and girls. So, enjoy a delicious bowl of Fruit of the Spirit Cocktail as often as you like.

Remember when you are at school to eat them so your day will go well.

Eat them at home so mom can tell.

Everyone will notice you have
become healthy and strong!

They will want to be near
you all the day long.

Although, you will grow
outwardly from head to toe.

It won't compare to the new
character in you that will show.

So, bless you and enjoy this

Fruit of the Spirit Cocktail!

Printed in the United States
by Baker & Taylor Publisher Services